Scenes Along The Road

Scenes Along the Road

Photographs of the Desolation Angels 1944-1960

Compiled by Ann Charters
with three poems and comments by Allen Ginsberg

City Lights Books
San Francisco

Scenes Along the Road was originally published in 1970 by Portents in conjunction with the Gotham Book Mart as part of its fiftieth-year celebration.

Cover photo hand-colored by Kim McCloud

Library of Congress Cataloging in Publication Data
Main entry under title

Scenes along the road.
    Reprint. Originally published: New York : Portents/
Gotham Book Mart, 1970.
      1. Bohemianism—United States—Pictorial works.
2. Authors, American—20th century—Portraits.
I. Ginsberg,Allen, 1926–
PS228.B6S28   1985   810'.9'0054 (B)   85-5763
ISBN 0-87286-168-6

CITY LIGHTS BOOKS are edited by Lawrence Ferlinghetti & Nancy J. Peters and published at the City Lights Bookstore, 261 Columbus Avenue, San Francisco, California 94133

CONTENTS

SCENES ALONG THE ROAD is a collection of snapshots of a group of men before they became, as Jack Kerouac put it, "famous writers more or less." In the 1940s and early 1950s, when most of the snapshots were taken, they were known only to each other, and these photos are candid shots they took to capture the private moments of their life and experience together. The collection begins with photos of Allen Ginsberg, Jack Kerouac, William Burroughs, Herbert Huncke, Gregory Corso, and John Clellon Holmes living in New York City shortly after World War II, engaged in an "adventurous education." The second section focuses on Neal Cassady, who came to New York from Denver in 1946 to meet Jack and Allen, and became the greatest influence on their life style and their writing. In the 1950s, when the scene shifted to San Francisco, the group included Gary Snyder, Philip Whalen, Michael McClure, and Lawrence Ferlinghetti, the period of Zen studies, poetry readings, and Berkeley parties. The last section of snapshots is from Mexico, Tangier, and Europe, the trips abroad before Kerouac and Ginsberg returned to the United States to be famous after the publication of *Howl, On the Road, Evergreen Review No. 2,* and *The New American Poetry*. The photos are drug store prints and "auto-portraits" taken for a quarter at bus stations, souvenirs of a life on the road. Now if they offer glimpses of a time past that looks as distant as our pre-history, it is only because these scenes have changed to become the present, and the road is now a familiar American highway.

The final section of the book contains three poems by Allen Ginsberg referring to people, places and times pictured in the photographs. The captions under the snapshots in quotation marks are also by Ginsberg. Longer quotations from the writing of Kerouac, Corso, Burroughs, Ginsberg, Snyder and Cassady are identified by the writer's name. All other text, and selection of photographs, is by Ann Charters.

This book is dedicated
to the memory of
Jack Kerouac
(1922-1969)

"I realized these were all the snapshots which our children would look at someday with wonder, thinking their parents had lived smooth, well-ordered, stabilized-within-the-photo lives and got up in the morning to walk proudly on the sidewalks of life, never dreaming the raggedy madness and riot of our actual lives, our actual night, the hell of it, the senseless emptiness. . . ."

—Is the Beat Generation a generation of outlaws? On what grounds do you presume to declare yourself exempt from your fellow humans?—
—Was the father of our country an outlaw? Yes. Was Galileo an outlaw for saying the world is round? I say the world is round! Not square! This is a fact.—

GREGORY CORSO

"Photo for M.S.T.S. training, Sheepshead Bay. Reading *War and Peace*. 1945."

Allen Ginsberg. "Poop of ship, Kearney-Baltimore run, 1945."

Ginsberg, like Kerouac, worked stints as a merchant seaman while at Columbia. Lucien Carr first brought them and Burroughs together in 1944.

"Jack Kerouac and Lucien Carr summer 1944, preparing to ship out to Paris. Then they got kicked off boat or quit boat and rushed down gangplank."

"Huncke summer 1947."

The writer Herbert Huncke was a close friend of Burroughs and character in his first book Junkie.

John Clellon Holmes, an early friend, whose novel Go *(1952) was the first to describe Ginsberg, Kerouac and Cassady.*

"One night in a dark empty bar sitting with my prison poems I was graced with a deep-eyed apparition: Allen Ginsberg. Through him I first learned about contemporary poesy. . . ." (1951)
Gregory Corso

Gregory Corso, Allen Ginsberg

In the winter, 1953, Burroughs came through New York on his way from South America to Tangier. He stayed with Ginsberg to edit their Yage letters. His novel Junkie, *written in Mexico City the previous year, had just appeared as a paperback ("Confessions of an Unredeemed Drug Addict"—"An ACE Original").*

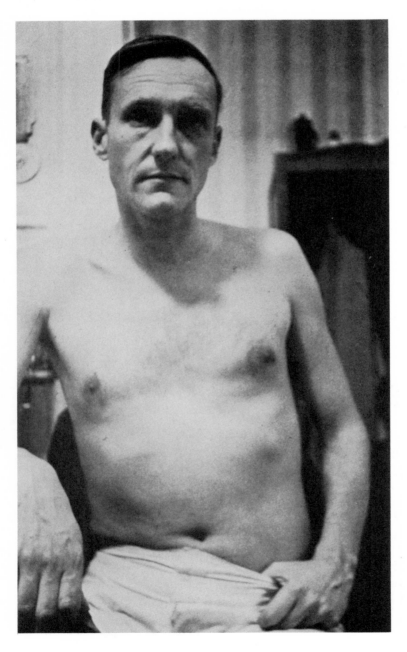

"Burroughs portrait by A.G. 1953. E. 7 St."

"N.Y. 1953. East 7 Street. Burroughs by A.G."

"Burroughs spent all his time talking and teaching others. . . . We all learned from him. He was a gray, non-descript-looking fellow you wouldn't notice on the street, unless you looked closer and saw his mad, bony skull with its strange youthfulness—a Kansas minister with exotic, phenomenal fires and mysteries."

Jack Kerouac

Burroughs and Kerouac, E. 7 St.

"A.G., W. S. Burroughs, Lucien Carr by Francesca Carr 1953. At L.C.'s Sheridan Square apartment."

A.G. "E. 7 St. 1953. Photo by Burroughs during editing of *Yage Letters*."

"J.K. and A.G."

"Jack on fire escape, E. 7 St. 1953. Photo by A. G. Note brakeman's handbook in jacket pocket, given Kerouac by Neal Cassady."

After four years working office jobs in New York Allen was very close to leaving for Mexico and California. Jack by this time had written On the Road, Visions of Cody, Doctor Sax, Maggie Cassady *and* The Subterraneans, *books only "published in heaven." Making his living as a railroad brakeman in California, he was growing bitter: "What the hell's the use?"*

HERE DOWN ON DARK EARTH
     before we all go to Heaven
VISIONS OF AMERICA
All that hitchhikin
All that railroadin
All that comin back
    to America
         JACK KEROUAC

"I.Q. 136-141 N. L. Cassady."

"N. Cassady in his first suit, bought in Chinatown, N.Y. 1946."

"Neal looking over autos, S.F. 1956."

Neal Cassady, hero of Kerouac's On the Road *and* Visions of Cody, *met Jack and Allen through Hal Chase in New York the summer of 1946. Jack lived on and off with Neal and his family in California during 1949-1956.*

"Neal, a good company man. Jack, the Communist. S.F. 1949."

Jack and Neal in California, 1949.

"Yes, and it wasn't only because I was a writer and needed new experiences that I wanted to know Neal more, and because my life hanging around the campus had reached the completion of its cycle and was stultified, but because, somehow, in spite of our differences in character, he reminded me of some long-lost brother. . . ."
                    Jack Kerouac

"Where's this guy Kerouac anyhow? Once in awhile he says something good, but usually just listens to me and sometimes grunts approval; at others asks something stupid — oh well, he's fun enough I guess and he does listen good. . . ."

Neal Cassady

Jack in California with the Cassadys, 1951.

Neal, Carolyn, and John Allen Cassady.

Carolyn Cassady: "Neal in heaven—an old car and a girl."

"Now you just dig them in front. They have worries, they're counting the miles, they're thinking about where to sleep tonight, how much money for gas, the weather, how they'll get there — and all the time they'll get there anyway, you see. But they need to worry and betray time with urgencies false and otherwise, purely anxious and whiny, their souls really won't be at peace unless they can latch on to an established and proven worry and having once found it they assume facial expressions to fit and go with it, which is, you see, unhappiness, and all the time it all flies by them and they know it and that *too* worries them no end."

Neal Cassady to Jack Kerouac

All afternoon cutting bramble blackberries off a tottering
brown fence
          under a low branch with its rotten old apricots miscellaneous
under the leaves. . . .
              ALLEN GINSBERG

"Formal portrait of Montgomery St. room, Bob LaVigne's paintings on wall, before or during composition of *Howl* summer 1955."

Allen, Montgomery St. room.

"Peter Orlovsky taken in front of giant visage portrait of himself by LaVigne. Probably Hotel Wentley 1955."

Allen and Peter.

"Peter makes me look at him, his intense wild face with that soft hawk nose and his blond hair crew cut now (before a wild shock) and his thick serious lips (like Allen's) but tall and lean and really only just outa high school."
Jack Kerouac

Gary Snyder.

". . . a bearded interesting Berkeley cat name of Snyder, I met him yesterday (via Rexroth suggestion) who is studying oriental and leaving in a few months on some privately put up funds to go be a Zen monk (a real one). He's a head, peyotlist, laconist, but warmhearted, nice looking with a little beard, thin, blond, rides a bicycle in Berkeley in red corduroy and levis and hungup on indians . . . Interesting person."
Allen Ginsberg, Sept. 9, 1955

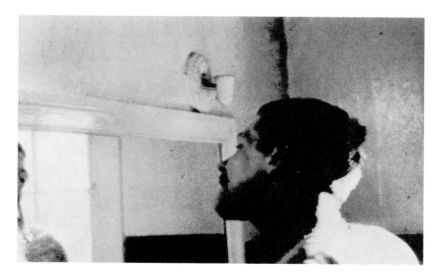

"Snapshot Snyder shaving Berkeley 1956."

"Snyder in garden outside his hut, Berkeley backyard, 1956."

"White-crowned sparrows
Make tremendous singings in the trees
The rooster down the valley crows and crows.
Jack Kerouac outside, behind my back
Reads the *Diamond Sutra* in the sun."
Gary Snyder ("These lines describe the cabin in Mill
Valley I lived in w/Kerouac Fall '55-
Spring '56." G.S.)

Michael McClure.

"Mike is one if not THE most handsome man I've ever seen—same dark-haired handsome slightly sliteyed look you expect from the myth appearance of Billy the Kid. . . ."
Jack Kerouac

Philip Whalen, Mohammed Hassan, Tom Jackrell.

Jack Kerouac, Lawrence Ferlinghetti.

"And on the way we drop in on Ferlinghetti at the bookstore and the idea suddenly comes to go to the cabin and spend a big quiet crazy weekend (how?) but when Larry hears this idea he'll come too . . . and we'll catch McClure at Santa Cruz and go visit Henry Miller and suddenly another big huge ball is begun."

Jack Kerouac

"Bob Donlin, Neal Cassady, A.G., Bob LaVigne, Larry Ferlinghetti in front of City Lights Bookstore, 1956. Photo by
Peter Orlovsky."

By plane, car, horse, camel, elephant, tractor, bicycle and steam roller, on foot, skis, sled, crutch and pogo-stick the tourists storm the frontiers, demanding with inflexible authority asylum from the "unspeakable conditions obtaining in Freeland," the Chamber of Commerce striving in vain to stem the debacle: "Please to be restful. It is only a few crazies who have from the crazy place outbroken."
WILLIAM BURROUGHS

"Jack K., Peter O., Bill B., Tangier, 1957."

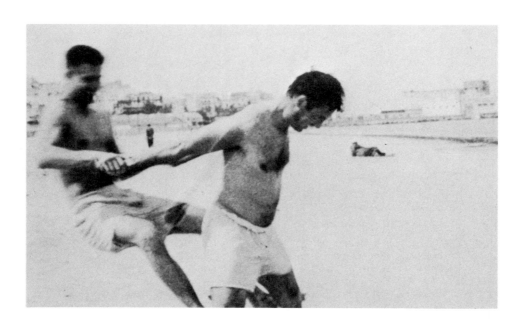

"Bill Burroughs. Tangier 1957 on beach, taken by Jack K."

"Moghreb is the Arab name of the country. . . . It was a little shoeshine boy on the beach who pronounced the name for me by spitting it out and giving me a fierce look then trying to sell me dirty pictures then rushing off to play soccer in the beach sand."
    Jack Kerouac

"August 1951, Chapultapec Park, Mexico City. Spent several weeks with Joan Burroughs."

A.G., 1954.

"Jack, Allen, Peter Orlovsky, Gregory Corso, Lafcadio Orlovsky, Mexico City Zocalo, 1956."

"People keep seeing destruction or rebellion in Jack's writing, and *Howl,* but that is a very minor element, actually; it only seems to be so to people who have accepted standard American values as permanent. What we are saying is that these values are not really standard nor permanent, and we are in a sense I think ahead of the times. . . . When you have a whole economy involved in some version of moneymaking—this just is no standard of values. That it seems to offer a temporary security may be enough to keep people slaving for it. But meanwhile it destroys real value. And it ultimately breaks down. Whitman long ago complained that unless the material power of America were leavened by some kind of spiritual infusion we would wind up among the 'fabled damned.' It seems we're approaching that state as far as I can see. Only way out is individuals taking responsibility and saying what they actually feel — which is an enormous human achievement in any society. That's just what we as a 'group' have been trying to do. To class that as some form of 'rebellion' in the kind of college-bred social worker doubletalk . . . misses the huge awful point."

Allen to Louis Ginsberg, Nov. 30. 1957

"A.G. on San Sammuele, Venice, 1957, by Peter O. Visiting Alan Ansen."

Gregory Corso, Alan Ansen.

"September 1957 summoned by my vision-agent
via ventriloquial telegram
delivered by the dumb mouths stoned upon Notre Dame
        given golden fare & 17th Century diagram
I left the gargoyle city
And
Two suitcases filled with despair
        arrived in Rotterdam. . . ."
        Gregory Corso

". . . what I've tried to be for a lot of people, that's the image I had of myself as Poet-prophet-friend on side of love & the Wild Good. That's the karma I wanted . . . that was the ideal mellow feeling I had respecting Kerouac and other Heroes for me, Neal, Bill, including Huncke; and anybody that dug that scene with us. Already it's an exclusive club. . . ."

Allen Ginsberg

Gregory Corso, Athens.

"L-R: Orlovsky, Burroughs, Ginsberg, Ansen, Bowles, Corso, Ian Summerville. Tangier, garden of Villa Mouneria where Burroughs lived."

"Jack in Tangier 1957, Villa Mouneria. Photo by Burroughs."

"At the time I sincerely believed that the only decent activity in the world was to pray for everyone, in solitude. I had many mystic joys on my roof, even while Bill or Allen were waiting for me downstairs. . . . in fact at that very moment the manuscript of *On the Road* was being linotyped for imminent publication and I was already sick of the whole subject."
                    Jack Kerouac

THREE POEMS BY ALLEN GINSBERG

John Clellon Holmes, Allen Ginsberg, Gregory Corso at Kerouac's grave, Lowell, Mass. Oct. 24, 1969.

Neal's Ashes

Delicate eyes that blinked blue Rockies all ash
nipples, ribs I touched w/ my thumb are ash
mouth my tongue touched once or twice all ash
bony cheeks soft on my belly are cinder, ash
earlobes & eyelids, youthful cock tip, curly pubis
breast warmth, man palm, high school thigh,
baseball bicept arm, asshole anneal'd to silken skin
                    all ashes, all ashes again.

August 1968

Memory Gardens

        covered with yellow leaves
           in morning rain

—Quel Deluge
      he threw up his hands
         & wrote the Universe don't exist
         & died to prove it.

Full Moon over Ozone Park
     Airport Bus rushing thru dusk to
          Manhattan,
Jack the Wizard in his
         grave at Lowell
for the first nite—
That Jack thru whose eyes I
      saw
     smog glory light
        gold over Manhattos' spires
will never see these
      chimnies smoking
anymore over statues of Mary
      in the graveyard

Black misted canyons
       rising over the bleak
           river
Bright doll-like ads
     for Esso Bread—
Replicas multiplying beards
      Farewell to the Cross—
Eternal fixity, the big headed
     wax painted Buddha doll
       pale resting incoffened—
Empty skulled New
     York streets
Starveling phantoms
    filling city—

Wax dolls walking park
                    Ave,
Light gleam in eye glass
Voice echoing thru Microphones
Grand Central Sailor's
                    arrival 2 decades later
                              feeling melancholy—
Nostalgia for Innocent World
            War II—
A million corpses running
            across 42'd street
Glass buildings rising higher
                    transparent
                              aluminum—
artificial trees, robot sofas,
            Ignorant cars—
One Way Street to Heaven
            by dark Institute's red brick
                    facade.

Grey Subway Roar

A wrinkled brown faced fellow
                    with swollen hands
leans to the blinking plate glass
            mirroring white poles, the heavy car
            sways on tracks uptown to Columbia—
Jack no more'll step off at Penn Station
            anonymous erranded, eat sandwich
            & drink beer near New Yorker Hotel or walk
under the shadow of Empire State.

Didn't we stare at each other length of the car
            & read headlines in faces thru Newspaper Holes?
Sexual cocked & horny bodied young, look
            at beauteous Rimbaud & Sweet Jenny
                    riding to class from Columbus Circle.
"Here the kindly dopefiend lived."

and the rednecked sheriff beat the longhaired
                    boy on the ass.
—103'd street, me & Hal abused for sidewalk begging.
Can I go back in time & lay my head on a teen age
            belly upstairs on 110'th Street?

or step off the iron car with Jack
    at the blue tiled Columbia sign?
at last the old brown station where I had
a holy vision's been rebuilt, clean ceramic
over the scum & spit & come of quarter century.

Saki Wani Choey Bhaki/Cupbearing kid where's the hash?

Flying to Maine in a trail of black smoke
Kerouac's obituary conserves Time's
        Front Paragraphs—
Empire State in Heaven Sun Set Red
      in old October, white mist
        over the billion trees of Bronx—
           There's too much to see—
Jack saw sun set red over Hudson horizon
        Two three decades back
thirtynine fourtynine fiftynine
        sixtynine
Smoke plumed up from oceanside chimnies
      plane roars toward Montauk
        stretched in red sunset—

Northport, in the trees, Jack drank
    rot gut & made haikus of birds
        tweetling on his porch rail at dawn—
Fell down and saw Death's golden lite
      in Florida garden a decade ago.
Now taken utterly, soul upward,
      & body down in wood coffin
        & concrete slab-box.
I threw a kissed handful of damp earth
      down on the stone lid
        & sighed
      looking in Creeley's one eye,
Peter sweet holding a flower
    Gregory toothless bending his
      knuckle to Cinema machine—
and that's the end of the drabble tongued
    Poet who sounded his Kock-rup
      throughout the Northwest Passage.
Blue dusk over Saybrook, Holmes
    sits down to dine Victorian—

& Time has a ten page spread on
    Homosexual-Fairies!

Well, while I'm here I'll
        do the work—
and what's the Work?
     To ease the pain of living.
Everything else, drunken
        dumbshow.

October 22-29, 1969

In a Car

Grey smoke cloud over Elmira,
The vast boy reformatory brick factory
Valed below misty hills 25 years ago
I sat with Lu visiting and murmured green Grass.
Jack's just not *here* anymore, Neal's ashes.
Loneliness makes old men moan, God's solitude,
O women shut up, yelling for baby meat more.

November 10, 1969